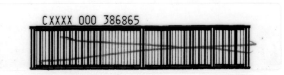

LET'S LOOK AT
WHALES

Malcolm Penny

Language consultant
Diana Bentley
University of Reading

Artist
Colin Newman

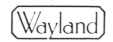

Wayland

Let's Look At

Aircraft

Bears

Big Cats

Bikes

Birds

Castles

Circuses

Colours

Dinosaurs

Farming

Horses

Monster Machines

Outer Space

Racing Cars

Rain

The Seasons

Sharks

Ships and Boats

Sunshine

Tractors

Trains

Trucks

Volcanoes

Whales

Editor: Anna Girling

First published in 1990 by
Wayland (Publishers) Ltd
61 Western Road, Hove
East Sussex BN3 1JD, England

British Library Cataloguing in Publication Data
Penny, Malcolm
    Let's look at whales.
    1. Whales
    I. Title II. Newman, Colin
    599'.5

ISBN 1-85210-833-9

Phototypeset by Kalligraphics Ltd, Horley, Surrey
Printed and bound by Casterman, S.A., Belgium

Words printed in
bold are explained
in the glossary

Contents

What is a whale?

Whales are huge animals that look like giant fish, but they are not fish at all! They are mammals.

All mammals have warm blood and they breathe air. They feed on milk from their mother.

Whales have no back legs, and instead of front legs they have **flippers**. Their tails have wide **flukes** at the side to help them swim. Whales keep warm by being covered in a thick layer of fat. This fat is called **blubber**.

Humpback whales

Whales with teeth and whales without teeth

There are two types of whale, some with teeth and some without.

Whales without teeth have **baleen** instead. Baleen is like a row of huge brushes in the whale's mouth. The whale takes a mouthful of water and spits it out through the brushes. The brushes trap the small animals that are in the water. The whale eats these animals for food.

Killer whale

Humpback whale

The small animals which whales eat are called krill. Krill are like shrimps. They swim in the water in enormous **swarms.**

Grey whale

The biggest whales of all

Blue whales are the biggest whales. They are the biggest animals that have ever lived on Earth. A blue whale can grow up to 30 metres long and can weigh more than 135 tonnes. It can be longer than a swimming pool and heavier than three large lorries.

Blue whales have baleen instead of teeth. They feed on krill and small fish. They have to catch many thousands of fish or millions of krill every day.

Singing whales

Humpback whales sing under water. The males growl and whistle so loudly that they can be heard by other whales many kilometres away. In the days before ships had engines, sailors lying in their **bunks** at night used to be able to hear the whales singing.

Humpback whales have baleen, not teeth. They live in warm seas in winter, but in summer they swim nearer the North or South Pole, where there is more food for them in the cold water.

Travelling whales

Grey whales travel very long distances every year. They swim thousands of kilometres, from near the North Pole to the coast of Mexico, to have their babies. People go out in small boats to see the whales. Some grey whales are so **tame** that they let people pat them.

Grey whales feed by scooping up mud from the bottom of shallow water, and then sieving it through their baleen.

Sperm whales

Sperm whales have teeth to catch their food. They can dive more than a kilometre deep and stay under water for more than an hour. They dive to catch **squid**, which are their main food.

In such deep water the squid are very big. Some of them have **tentacles** over 10 metres long.

Sperm whales are the biggest whales with teeth. They usually grow to about 18 metres long and weigh about 45 tonnes.

Killer whales

People used to think that killer whales were very fierce and dangerous. Now we know that they are quite gentle and intelligent.

Killer whales have teeth. They feed mostly on fish but also eat seals, penguins and porpoises.

Killer whales live in families, called **pods**. The families keep together by making whistling sounds to each other. When they hunt they make buzzing sounds. The sounds bounce off fish in the sea so that the whale can hear where its food is.

Pilot whales

Pilot whales were given their name by fishermen who believed they would show them the way to where the best fish could be caught. They are black and only about 6 metres long, which is small for a whale. Sailors often see pilot whales in the Atlantic Ocean.

Pilot whales are very friendly to people. At one time the American Navy trained them to fetch things from the bottom of the sea.

Pilot whales have teeth. They can dive very deep to find squid to eat.

The smallest whales

The smallest whales are porpoises and dolphins. There are many different types living in different places all over the world.

Dolphins are very playful animals. They often jump out of the water, spinning round or turning cartwheels. They are friendly and easy to tame. Sometimes they are kept in **captivity** so that people can watch them performing tricks.

Dolphins and porpoises can swim very fast. This helps them to catch fish in their sharp teeth.

A whale is born

It is very unusual to see a whale being born because this normally happens out at sea or in a small bay where people do not go. Once, in America, a killer whale mother gave birth to her baby in a big pool where people could watch.

As the baby's head appeared, the mother rolled over and over in the water until the baby popped out. The baby could swim straight away and soon went to the surface of the pool to take its first breath of air. The baby was over 2 metres long.

Captive whales

A pool where whales and dolphins are kept in captivity is called a dolphinarium. The biggest whales to be kept in a dolphinarium are killer whales and pilot whales. Many people think that it is cruel to keep such big animals in a pool.

However, dolphins seem to be quite happy in captivity. They become very tame and people like to watch them. A lot of what we know about whales comes from watching captive dolphins.

Whales and people

Long ago, American Indians hunted whales for food and for their blubber, which they melted to make oil. They went out in **canoes** and would only kill one whale, leaving the others.

Later, whale oil became very valuable. Men came in large ships to kill the whales. Soon they had killed many thousands of them, until there were very few left.

Whaling has almost stopped now. We do not need to hunt whales because we can get oil from other sources. Sadly, people from some countries still kill whales.

Can the whales come back?

Grey whales have recovered from whaling. There are now almost as many of them as there were before whaling started. Other great whales, like blue whales and humpback whales, are still very **rare**.

In the Antarctic, near the South Pole, where whales were once very common, other animals like to eat krill. There are now more penguins and seals because there has been plenty of food for them while so many whales were being killed. Now that the penguins and seals are eating the krill, there might not be enough for the whales.

Can the big whales come back? We shall have to wait and see.

Glossary

Baleen   The row of brushes which a whale without teeth uses to catch its food.

Blubber   The layer of fat which keeps a whale warm.

Bunk   A bed on a ship.

Canoe   A small light boat used by Indians.

Captivity   This means keeping a wild animal in a cage or pool.

Flippers   A whale's front legs, which are shaped like paddles to help it swim.

Flukes   The flaps on the sides of a whale's tail.

Pod   The name for a group of whales.

Rare   Not often seen, very few in number.

Squid   An animal like an octopus, but with ten legs instead of eight.

Swarm   A large crowd of small animals, like ants or bees. Large crowds of krill are called swarms.

Tame   Gentle, not wild.

Tentacles   The rubbery 'arms' of a squid, which it uses when feeding.

Whaling   Hunting for whales, for food or for their blubber.

Books to read

Whales and Dolphins, Lionel
    Bender (Franklin Watts,
    1988)
Whales and Dolphins,
    Terence Wise (Wayland,
    1980)
Whales of the World, Lyall
    Watson (Hutchinson,
    1981)
A Year in the Life of a Whale,
    John Stidworthy
    (Macdonald, 1987)

Index